Stop That Popcorn!

Written by Catherine Baker
Illustrated by Neil Sutherland, Blue-Zoo and Tony Trimmer

C rubs her tum.

P needs a snack too.

or!

or!

Then O and R turn into OR.

We can help you. Join up with us!

p-**o**-**p**-**c**-**or**-**n**, popcorn!
They get a big pan.

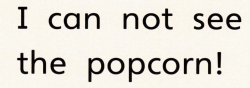

I can not see the popcorn!

Can I look in the pan?

No! You will spoil the popcorn!

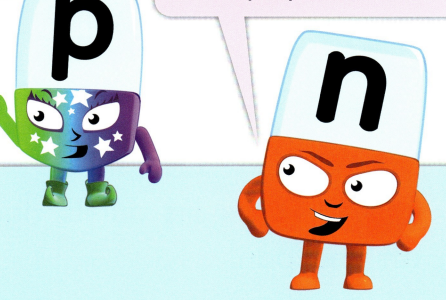

But then the lid bursts right off the pan!

C and N help P, but
the popcorn keeps popping.

A and R join up and get AR.

c-ar-t-o-n, carton!
They get a big carton.

They fill the carton
with popcorn.

The pan stops popping.